Living History

Frontier Fort

Fort Life on the Upper Mississippi, 1826

by Megan O'Hara
Photography by Tim Rummelhoff

Content Consultants
Stephen Osman, Site Manager
Thomas Shaw, Asst. Site Manager
Historic Fort Snelling

Blue Earth Books
an imprint of Capstone Press

Blue Earth Books
818 North Willow Street, Mankato, Minnesota 56001
http://www.capstone-press.com

Library of Congress Cataloging-in-Publication Data
O'Hara, Megan.
    Frontier fort: fort life on the upper Mississippi, 1826/by Megan O'Hara.
    p. cm.--(Living History)
    Includes bibliographical references (p. 30) and index.
    Summary: Provides a look at the history and importance of one particular frontier fort and
describes what life was like for its inhabitants.
    ISBN 1-56065-725-1
    1. Fort Snelling (Minn.)--History--Juvenile literature. 2. Frontier and pioneer life--
Minnesota--Fort Snelling--Juvenile literature. [1.Frontier and pioneer life--Minnesota. 2. Fort
Snelling (Minn.)] I. Title. II. Series: Living History (Mankato, Minn.)
F614.F7089   1998
977.6'57--dc21   97-31877
                                      CIP
                                      AC

Editorial credits:

Editor, Christy Steele; design, Patricia Bickner Linder; illustrations, Timothy Halldin

Photo credits:

Minnesota Historical Society/Phil Hutchins, 26
All other photographs by Tim Rummelhoff

Contents

Acknowledgments

We are grateful to the following for the contribution of their time, knowledge, and expertise and for the use of the Fort Snelling site and artifacts: Stephen Osman, site manager; Thomas Shaw, assistant site manager; and Laurie Brickley and Liz Turchin of the Minnesota Historical Society. These Fort Snelling interpreters we gratefully acknowledge for their patience and help: Matthew Buhaug, Gerald Fritsch, David Grabitske, Matthew Hutchinson, Nick Jeter, Spencer Johnson, Merideth Kessler, Amy Kruger, Griffin Larson, Pam Larson, Pamela Larson, Peter Laughlin, Kirsten Theis Ben Lee, Karla Myers, Keith Nelson, Jeffery Nordin, Michael Olander, Laurel Osman, Jennifer Pansch, Paul Pederson, Eva Quigley, Thomas Sanders, Sam Severson, Bridget Sexton, Thomas Shaw, Winona Siyaka, and Andrew Timmer.

Location of Fort Snelling
St. Paul, Minnesota

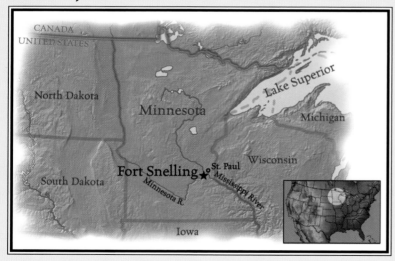

**This map of Fort St. Anthony was made in 1823.
The fort was renamed Fort Snelling in 1825.**

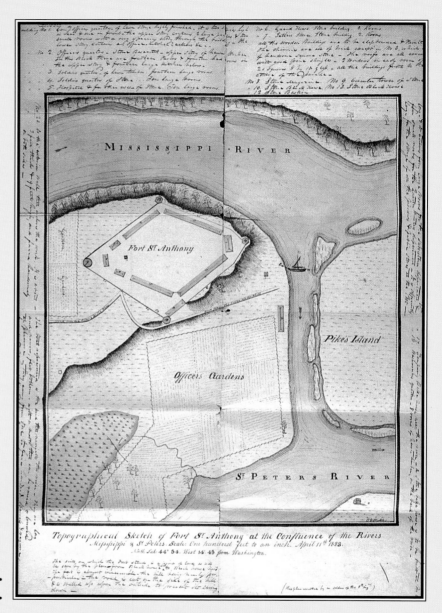

Introduction

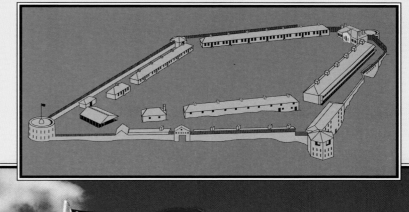

In 1826, Fort Snelling was a busy gathering place for fur traders and American Indians. It was the last place people could stop for supplies before entering the wilderness. U.S. soldiers built the fort on high land that overlooked where the Mississippi and Minnesota Rivers meet.

Many people lived inside the fort. Most were soldiers and their families. Soldiers had many jobs. They performed their military duties and maintained the fort. They planted and harvested the fort's corn and vegetable crops. The crops were important foods for everybody living at the fort. Soldiers also fished in the nearby rivers.

Some soldiers had special skills. They supplied needed services to people in the area. A soldier doctor ran the fort's hospital. A soldier blacksmith made shoes for horses and oxen. The blacksmith also made and fixed metal tools. Soldier carpenters made needed items like furniture out of wood.

Soldiers' wives sometimes lived at the fort, too. These women had many jobs. They did laundry by hand, taught children, sewed clothing, cooked meals, and grew vegetable gardens.

Fur traders and Dakota Indians came from surrounding areas to camp outside the fort's walls. The fur traders established outposts throughout the wilderness. At the outposts, they traded goods for animal furs or pelts. Dakota people brought many pelts to the fur traders. There were two large fur trade companies near Fort Snelling.

There were many Dakota Indian villages near the fort. Dakota Indians are also called Sioux Indians. In the summer, they lived in elm bark homes. They planted vegetable gardens. The Dakota lived in tepees during hunting season. Tepees were homes made of poles that were covered with animal skins. The Dakota could easily take down and move their tepees. They moved their villages several times each year.

Dakota Indians were important to fort life. They came to the fort to trade. They sometimes brought wild rice, maple syrup, or fresh buffalo meat or deer meat to the fort. This was one of the few ways people living in the fort obtained these foods.

The land around the fort belonged to the American Indians. It was called Indian Territory. Soldiers made sure that settlers did not take land owned by the American Indians. The fort's soldiers also helped protect settlers who were traveling through Indian Territory.

7

A Frontier Fort in the 1800s

My name is Henry Snelling, and I am 10 years old. I live here at Fort Snelling with my mother and father. My father is the commander of the fort. There was only wilderness when we first moved here in 1820. Our family and the soldiers lived in tents until the fort was finished. My father designed the fort, and the soldiers built it. Father did such a good job that the military named the fort after him. This is what the fort looks like today.

Reveille

Every morning the soldiers play music called reveille to wake up everyone in the fort. My little brother James wants to keep sleeping. Not me. There are too many things to see and do. The blacksmith promised that I would get my new ax today. I am eager to try it out.

The cook and servants are busy in the kitchen downstairs. The pans rattle as the servants prepare breakfast. If I hurry, I can watch the soldiers raise the flag.

I am reminded that the fort is more than just my home when I watch the soldiers raise the U.S. flag. People come inside the fort for protection in times of war. It is the soldiers' job to protect us. These men also tend the crops and fish with me. I sometimes forget that someday they could lose their lives trying to save mine.

I have to hurry back and get dressed. Father will not be pleased if I am late for breakfast.

cap

shirt

roundabout

pantaloons

This is the clothing I wear during the day: shirt, pantaloons, roundabout, and cap.

Breakfast

My family gathers at the breakfast table each morning. Barbara Ann lives with us and helps take care of us. My friend John Tulley joins us, too. John lives with us. The Sisseton Dakota Indians killed his parents when they were traveling through Indian territory. John lived with the Indians for awhile. But the Indian agent gave money to the Dakota for John's release. John then came to live with us in the fort. His brother Andrew lives with the Clarks. The Clarks live in the fort, too.

At breakfast we talk about our plans for the day. Father will be meeting with his Dakota friend, Chief Wanata. Three of the officers' wives are coming to drink tea with my mother. Mother's name is Abigail Snelling. I plan to visit the blacksmith to pick up my ax. But first James, John, and I must go to school. This is the last thing I feel like doing today. I hope the schoolmaster is in a good humor.

Frontier Schools

There were often no schools or teachers on the frontier. The school at Fort Snelling was the first school in what is now Minnesota. Sometimes there was no teacher at the fort school. Officers' wives would then teach their children in their homes. Sometimes officers would send their children to schools in other states. Poor children often had no schooling.

Unlike today's schools, frontier schools did not have textbooks. Books were very expensive. Students brought any books their parents owned to school.

Students studied arithmetic, reading, writing, penmanship, grammar, spelling, and geography.

There was not much paper in those days. Children had blackboard slates. They wrote on the slates instead of paper. Students often memorized long passages of poetry or Bible verses. They recited the passages to the teacher.

School

Our schoolmaster is strict. He makes us stay after school if we misbehave, and sometimes he tells our parents.

We must memorize Bible verses for reading class. The schoolmaster calls us to the front of the room. Then we must say our verses out loud for him. My verses are from the book of Proverbs.

The verses are very long. I worked hard to memorize them. But the other students' chatter makes me lose my thoughts. The schoolmaster corrects me sternly when I get stuck.

This morning we will also learn grammar, spelling, and elocution. Elocution is a fancy word for speaking well and persuasively in front of a group.

Dinner

At noon it is time for dinner. We enjoy the warm weather outside during our break. Some people bring their meals to school in dinner pails. I go home for dinner every day. I hope the Indian agent Major Taliaferro will join us today. He always has good stories to tell.

Malcolm, John, and I wrestle before school begins again. We do not look forward to an afternoon of school. We will have to sit still for geography and arithmetic lessons.

After school my friends tease me about my mistakes during lessons. I challenge them to a hoop and stick race. This is one of our favorite games.

Play Hoop and Stick

Hoops were favorite toys in the 1800s. Metal hoops came from barrels. Adults took the barrels apart to get the hoops. Other adults made wooden hoops for children.

Children used sticks to push and roll their hoops. Some children could make their hoops do special tricks. They used their sticks to make their hoops twist and turn. You can have a hoop and stick race.

What You Need
One hula hoop per player
One thick stick per player

What You Do
1. Pick a starting line and a finishing line for the race.
2. Have all the players line up behind the starting line.
3. Have someone give the signal to start.
4. Use your sticks to keep the hoops rolling and moving forward.
5. If a player's hoop falls to the ground, that player must return to the starting line and start over.
6. The first player to cross the finish line is the winner.

Blacksmith

After the race, Malcolm, John, and I visit Private Christian. He is the blacksmith in the fort. We are just in time to watch him forge my ax.

The blacksmith shop is hot and dark. The fire makes it sooty and smoky. Still, it is one of my favorite places in the fort. Private Christian pumps the huge bellows to make the fire hotter. The bellows blows air into the fire.

Next, Private Christian places the metal in the fire. It soon glows orange with the heat. This means the metal is ready to be shaped. The blacksmith places the metal on his anvil. He pounds it with a hammer to shape the ax head.

I can do a lot of things with my new ax. I can cut down small tamarack trees to get the sticky gum. The gum will help seal the cracks in my canoe.

I thank Private Christian for my ax. Malcolm, John, and I hurry outside. We are going fishing.

Make a Fishing Pole

What You Need

One long, sturdy stick
Twine
Scissors
A hook
Worms or other things
for bait

What You Do

1. Cut a long piece of twine.
2. Tie the twine to the stick. Make sure the twine is tied tightly.
3. Tie the hook to the loose end of the twine.
4. Put the bait on the hook.

You are now ready to go fishing.

Fishing

Fishing is one of our favorite things to do. Today is warm and beautiful. It is a perfect day for catching fish. The Mississippi River is just below the fort. The river is full of catfish, pike, and bass.

My friends and I made our fishing poles out of willow branches and twine. We use salt pork for bait.

The fish are hungry for the salt pork today.
Mother will be pleased with our catch. I will ask
her if we can eat the fish for our supper.

John tells the story about when I fell in the river
last year. I nearly drowned. It was not funny when
it happened, but I can smile about it now.

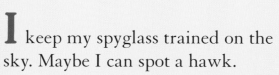

I keep my spyglass trained on the
sky. Maybe I can spot a hawk.

Weaving

I meet my friends Charlotte Clark and Winona. Winona is our Dakota Indian friend from a nearby village. Charlotte and I watch Winona fingerweave.

Winona is making fancy garters to hold up her father's leggings. Her fingers move quickly through the yarn strands. Charlotte and I are learning how to fingerweave. Winona patiently shows us the steps.

Fur Trade Game

American Indians often used pelts instead of money on the frontier. Most people traded muskrat pelts for small goods. Muskrat pelts were usually worth 20 cents.

American Indian traders used muskrat pelts to purchase the following goods at the American Fur Company post in 1827. You can figure out the money value for each item.

One breechcloth costs
   10 muskrat pelts

One print shirt costs
   20 muskrat pelts

One blanket costs
   40 muskrat pelts

One measure of gun powder costs
   10 muskrat pelts

One knife costs
   two muskrat pelts

Dakota Indians

Many fur traders and Dakota Indians visit Fort Snelling. The Dakota trade animal pelts to the fur traders for blankets, fabrics, and tools.

Father and Chief Wanata are walking together outside the fort walls. Chief Wanata once planned an attack on Fort Snelling, but Father made peace. There was no bloodshed. Now Chief Wanata and Father respect each other. They work together as allies. Other Dakota chiefs like Black Dog are also Father's allies. This helps Father keep peace between the Indian people and the white people.

I hope Chief Wanata and his men had success hunting buffalo. There might be some fresh buffalo meat for us tonight. My stomach rumbles just thinking about a tasty roast.

Dakota and Buffalo

Dakota Indians were known for their hunting skills. They moved their villages several times a year to hunt.

Dakota Indians mainly hunted buffalo. They used every part of the buffalo. They made clothes, blankets, and tepee covers out of buffalo skins. They made buffalo horns into bowls and cups. They shaped buffalo bones into tools and made brushes with buffalo hair.

Buffalo was an important food for Dakota people. Dakota women made jerky by drying buffalo meat. They also made pemmican by pounding the dried meat into a powder. They added berries and melted fat. Pemmican stayed fresh for many years.

Sutler's Store

Mother asked me to buy some sugar. I stop by the sutler's store before going home. The sutler is a storekeeper who sells all kinds of goods in the fort's store. The sutler's store is the only store in the fort. It has everything people might need, like fresh butter, dried apples, clothing, fabric, tools, and hardware.

The sutler writes down the cost of the sugar in his account book. Father pays our account a few times each year. The paymaster, Thomas Biddle, comes only two or three times each year. This is when all the soldiers receive their pay.

Sunday School

We have our Sunday School in my house on Sunday morning. My Mother and Mrs. Clark teach us lessons from the Bible. They listen to us read Bible verses.

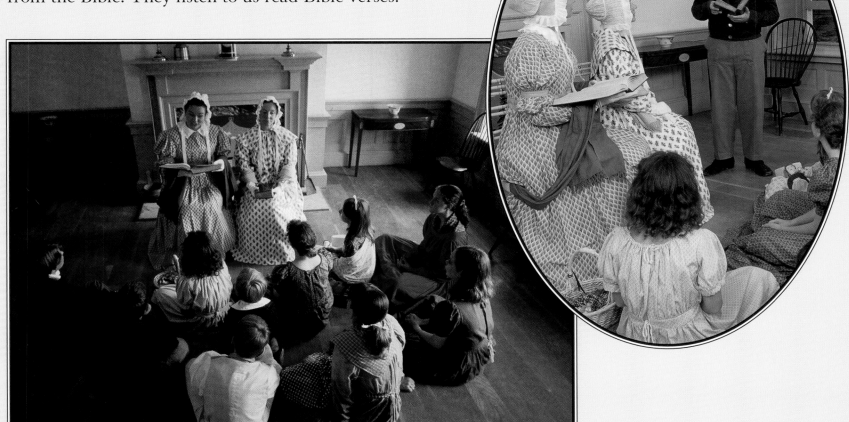

Evening

Father is busy during the day with his military duties. Sometimes in the evenings he reads with me.

The sentinel is a soldier who guards the fort. He calls out that all is well. Soon, it will be time for me to go to bed. Tomorrow's reveille will come at dawn.

Words to Know

ally (AL-eye)—a person or country that gives support to another person or country

anvil (AN-vuhl)—a large steel block with a flat top on which metal is shaped

bellows (BEL-ohss)—an instrument whose sides are squeezed to pump air into something such as a fire

breechcloth (BRICH-kloth)—a piece of deerskin or woolen cloth that passed between the legs and was tied around the waist with a belt

elocution (el-uh-KYOO-shuhn)—the art of speaking clearly and persuasively in front of a group

forge (FORJ)—to make or to form

garter (GAR-tur)—a band worn to keep a legging or stocking up

pantaloon (pan-tuh-LOON)—pants or trousers

pelt (PELT)—an animal's skin with the hair or fur still on it

reveille (RE-vuh-lee)—the military's musical signal to get up in the morning

roundabout (ROUN-duh-bout)—a short, close-fitting jacket

spyglass (SPYE-glass)—a small telescope; it makes faraway objects appear larger and closer

sutler (SUHT-luhr)—a storekeeper who had a shop in a military post

tepee (TEE-pee)—a house made of poles that are covered by animal skins

To Learn More

Bacon, Melvin and Daniel Blegen. *Bent's Fort: Crossroads of Cultures on the Santa Fe Trail*. Brookfield, Conn.: The Millbrook Press, 1995.

Kalman, Bobbie and David Schimpky. *Fort Life*. New York: Crabtree Publishing, 1994.

Lund, Bill. *The Sioux Indians*. Mankato, Minn.: Capstone Press, 1998.

Sneve, Virginia Driving Hawk. *The Sioux*. New York: Holiday House, 1993.

Internet Sites

Historic Forts
http://www.coax.net/people/lwf/wf_forts.htm

Living History Re-enactor Net
http://www.reenactor.net/

Minnesota Historical Society
http://www.mnhs.org/sites/snelling

Places to Write and Visit

Arkansas
Fort Smith
P.O. Box 1406
Fort Smith, AR 72902

California
Fort Point National Historic Site
Presidio of San Francisco, Bldg 989
San Francisco, CA 94129

Fort Guijarros Museum
P.O. Box 231500
San Diego, CA 92194

Sutter's Fort State Historic Park
802 North Street
Sacramento, CA 95814

Colorado
Bent's Old Fort National Historic Site
35110 Highway 194 East
La Junta, CO 81050-9523

Florida
Fort Caroline National Memorial
12713 Fort Caroline Rd.
Jacksonville, FL 32225

Castillo de San Marcos
One South Castillo Drive
St. Augustine, FL 32084

Fort Jefferson
Dry Tortugas National Park
P.O. Box 6208
Key West, FL 33041

Florida
Fort George State Cultural Site
c/o The Talbot Islands GEO Park
11435 East Fort George Road
Fort George, FL 32226

Georgia
Fort Pulaski
P.O. Box 30757
U.S. Highway 80 East
Savannah, GA 31410-0757

Kansas
Fort Scott National Historic Site
Old Fort Boulevard
Fort Scott, KS 66701-1471

Maryland
**Fort McHenry National Monument
and Historic Shrine**
2400 East Fort Avenue
Baltimore, MD 21230

Michigan
Colonial Michilimackinac
P.O. Box 873
Mackinaw City, MI 44701

Minnesota
Fort Snelling
Fort Snelling History Center
St. Paul, MN 55111-4060

Nebraska
Fort Kearny
Nebraska State Historical Society
Kearney, NE 68848

New Hampshire
Fort at No. 4 Living History Museum
RR 11, Springfield Road
P.O. Box 336
Charlestown, NH 03603

New Mexico
Fort Union National Monument
P.O. Box 127
Watrous, NM 87753

New York
Castle Clinton
26 Wall Street
New York, NY 10005

Old Fort Niagara
P.O. Box 169
Youngstown, NY 14174-0169

North Dakota
Fort Union Trading Post
RR 3, Box 71
Williston, ND 58801

Oregon
Fort Clatsop
RR 3, Box 604-FC
Astoria, OR 97103

South Carolina
Fort Sumter
1214 Middle Street
Sullivan's Island, SC 29482

Texas
Fort Lancaster State Historical Park
P.O. Box 306
Sheffield, TX 79781

The Alamo
300 Alamo Plaza
San Antonio, TX 78205

Fort Richardson State Historical Park
P.O. Box 4
Jacksboro, TX 76458

Washington
Fort Vancouver National Historic Site
612 East Reserve Street
Vancouver, WA 98661

Wyoming
Fort Bridger State Historic Site
P.O. Box 35
Fort Bridger, WY 82933

Fort Laramie National Historic Site
HC 72, Box 389
Fort Laramie, WY 82212

Canada
Old Fort William
Box 165
Vicker's Heights, ON P0T 2Z0
Canada

Fort George & Buckingham House
Provincial Historic Site
Secondary Road 646
Alberta 2L5 06D
Canada

About Fort Snelling

The military used Fort Snelling for more than 125 years. People built new barracks, officers' quarters, and storehouses between 1880 and the early 1900s. At this time, the soldiers tore down the buildings of the old stone fort.

The military used the fort as a training post during the Civil War (1861-1865), World War I (1914-1918), and World War II (1939-1945). They stopped using the fort after World War II.

Minnesota wanted to build a freeway on the Fort Snelling site in the 1950s. People fought to save the old fort. Their work helped Fort Snelling become Minnesota's first National Historic Landmark in 1960. The Minnesota Historical Society rebuilt Fort Snelling in the 1960s and 1970s.

Today, Fort Snelling is surrounded by freeways and a large urban population. Within its walls, costumed guides called interpreters act out what it was like to be part of early military, civilian, and Dakota Indian life in the area. For more information, call the Minnesota Historical Society at 612-726-1171 or visit the society's Internet site at <http://www.mnhs.org>.